A Trip to the Park

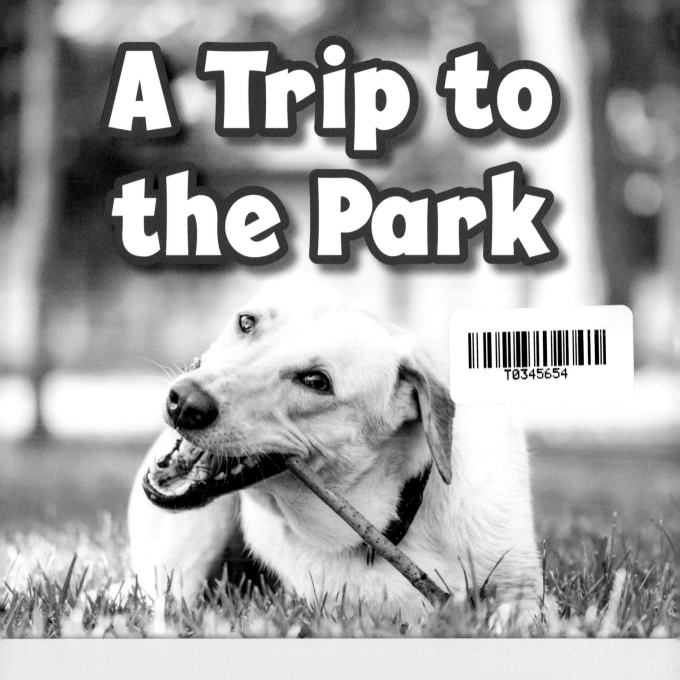

Written by Charmaine Foord

Do you like to go to the park?
There is so much to see and do!

We go when the sun is out.
My sister sits in her pram.

It is spring. There are lots of flowers and the grass is green.

Dogs like to go to the park.
They bark and pick up sticks.

I like the duck pond. In spring there are little ducklings!

The ducks quack when you feed them crusts.

Frogs jump in and out of the pond.
Splash!

They turn and hop when you
come near.

little swing

big swing

In this park there is a big swing
and a little swing.

I go on the big swing and see how high I can go!

In the corner of the park there is some woodland.

It is darker under the trees. Sunlight cannot get past the branches.

tree trunk

In the woods, I hunt for insects.
I inspect tree trunks.

I feel the bark of the trees. Some
bark is smooth and some is not.

What will you see at the park near you?